DOLPH ZIGGLER

BY NICK GORDON

BELLWETHER MEDIA · MINNEAPOLIS, MN

Are you ready to take it to the extreme?
Torque books thrust you into the action-packed world
of sports, vehicles, mystery, and adventure. These books
may include dirt, smoke, fire, and dangerous stunts.
WARNING : read at your own risk.

Library of Congress Cataloging-in-Publication Data

Gordon, Nick.
 Dolph Ziggler / by Nick Gordon.
    p. cm. -- (Torque: pro wrestling champions)
 Includes bibliographical references and index.
  ISBN 978-1-60014-783-8 (hardcover : alk. paper)
 1. Ziggler, Dolph, 1980---Juvenile literature. 2. Wrestlers--United States--Biography--Juvenile
literature. I. Title.
 GV1196.Z54G67 2012
 796.812092--dc23   2011052614

This edition first published in 2013 by Bellwether Media, Inc.

Printed in the United States of America, North Mankato, MN.

A special thanks to Devin Chen, John Smolek, and David Seto for contributing images.

CONTENTS

HEATED RIVALRY...................4

WHO IS
DOLPH ZIGGLER? 8

BECOMING A CHAMPION....16

GLOSSARY..............................22

TO LEARN MORE 23

INDEX....................................24

WARNING!

The wrestling moves used in this book are performed
by professionals. Do not attempt to reenact any
of the moves performed in this book.

HEATED RIVALRY

The fans booed Dolph Ziggler as he stepped into the ring. He was facing Kofi Kingston for the World Wrestling Entertainment (WWE) United States Championship. The two were bitter **rivals**. Ziggler came out strong. He had Kingston in a Sleeper Hold twice, but Kingston escaped each time.

KOFI
KINGSTON

VITAL STATS

Wrestling Name: _ _ _ _ _ _ _ _ _ _ _ Dolph Ziggler

Real Name: _ _ _ _ _ _ Nicholas Theodore Nemeth

Height: _ _ _ _ _ _ _ _ _ _ _ _ _ _ _ 6 feet (1.8 meters)

Weight: _ _ _ _ _ _ _ _ 213 pounds (97 kilograms)

Started Wrestling: _ _ _ _ _ _ _ _ _ _ _ _ _ _ _ 2004

Finishing Move: _ _ _ _ _ _ _ _ _ _ _ _ _ _ _ Zig-Zag

Kingston hit Ziggler with a **Diving Crossbody**. Ziggler was dazed. His manager reached into the ring and attacked Kingston. Ziggler put Kingston in yet another Sleeper Hold. Kingston could not escape this time. The referee ended the match. Ziggler was the new WWE United States Champion!

WHO IS DOLPH ZIGGLER?

Nicholas Theodore Nemeth was born on July 27, 1980 in Cleveland, Ohio. At a young age, Nemeth enjoyed wrestling, boxing, and **mixed martial arts**. He later became a star on his high school wrestling team. He set a school record with 82 pins in his career.

QUICK HIT!

Nemeth wrestled in the 165-pound (75-kilogram) class in college. He won three Mid-American Conference titles at that weight.

In 2000, Nemeth went to Kent State University. He studied **political science**. He also set a school wrestling record with 121 victories. Nemeth was planning on going to law school. Instead, he decided to follow his dream to become a professional wrestler.

Nemeth tried out for WWE in 2004. The company offered him a **developmental contract**. He wrestled in a small league called Ohio Valley Wrestling (OVW). In 2005, WWE officials decided Nemeth was ready to compete against WWE's best wrestlers.

Nemeth made his WWE television **debut** in 2005. In 2006, he wrestled as a member of the Spirit Squad. The group dressed as male cheerleaders. They learned their moves from real cheerleaders and **gymnasts**. Nemeth went back to smaller wrestling leagues when the group broke up.

QUICK HIT!

The Spirit Squad won the World Tag Team Championship in 2006.

BECOMING A CHAMPION

Nemeth returned to WWE in 2008. He wrestled as a **heel** named Dolph Ziggler. He defeated Kofi Kingston for the WWE Intercontinental Championship in the summer of 2010. In 2011, he won both the World Heavyweight Championship and the WWE United States Championship.

QUICK HIT!

In February 2011, Ziggler held the World Heavyweight Championship for 11 minutes and 23 seconds. He then lost it to Edge. It is one of the shortest title reigns in WWE history.

SLEEPER
HOLD

18

Ziggler has a wide range of **signature moves**. One is the Sleeper Hold. Ziggler wraps his arm around an opponent's neck until the opponent passes out. Ziggler also uses the Powerslam. He puts one arm under the opponent's legs and the other over his chest. Then he scoops the opponent up and slams him to the mat.

ZIG-ZAG

the Zig-Zag. He stands behind his opponent and leaps into the air. He grabs the opponent's head as he falls to the ground. The opponent's head slams hard into the mat. The Zig-Zag shows off Ziggler's speed, power, and athletic ability. It has made him one of WWE's rising stars.

QUICK HIT!

Ziggler once did a Zig-Zag to Christian off a ladder!

GLOSSARY

debut—a first appearance

developmental contract—an agreement in which a wrestler signs with WWE but then wrestles in a smaller league to gain experience and develop skills

Diving Crossbody—a move in which a wrestler launches off the top rope and slams his body into his opponent's chest

finishing move—a wrestling move meant to finish off an opponent so that he can be pinned

gymnasts—athletes who practice gymnastics; gymnasts use balance, strength, and control to perform moves.

heel—a wrestler seen by fans as a villain

mixed martial arts—a combat sport that combines a wide range of fighting styles

political science—the study of systems of government and power

rivals—competitors who are in a heated, long-lasting conflict

signature moves—moves that a wrestler is famous for performing

TO LEARN MORE

AT THE LIBRARY

Black, Jake. *The Ultimate Guide to WWE.* New York,
N.Y.: Grosset & Dunlap, 2011.

Gordon, Nick. *Kofi Kingston.* Minneapolis, Minn.:
Bellwether Media, 2012.

Kaelberer, Angie Peterson. *Cool Pro Wrestling Facts.*
Mankato, Minn.: Capstone Press, 2011.

ON THE WEB

Learning more about Dolph Ziggler
is as easy as 1, 2, 3.

1. Go to www.factsurfer.com.

2. Enter "Dolph Ziggler" into the search box.

3. Click the "Surf" button and you will see a list of
related Web sites.

With factsurfer.com, finding more information
is just a click away.

INDEX

Christian, 21

Cleveland, Ohio, 9

debut, 15

developmental contract, 12

Diving Crossbody, 7

Edge, 17

finishing move, 7, 21

gymnasts, 15

heel, 16

Kent State University, 11

Kofi Kingston, 4, 6, 7, 16

Ohio Valley Wrestling (OVW), 12

political science, 11

Powerslam, 19

rivals, 4

signature moves, 19

Sleeper Hold, 4, 7, 18, 19

Spirit Squad, 15

World Heavyweight Championship, 16, 17

World Tag Team Championship, 15

World Wrestling Entertainment (WWE), 4, 7, 12, 15, 16, 17, 21

WWE Intercontinental Championship, 16

WWE United States Champion, 7

WWE United States Championship, 4, 16

Zig-Zag, 7, 20, 21